Praying
with the
Psalms

3-Minute Devotions for Advent
and Christmas 2025

DEACON JASON BULMAN

AVE MARIA PRESS AVE Notre Dame, Indiana

Nihil Obstat:	Reverend Monsignor Michael Heintz, PhD
	Censor Librorum
Imprimatur:	Most Reverend Kevin C. Rhoades
	Bishop of Fort Wayne–South Bend
	Given at Fort Wayne, Indiana, on April 22, 2025

Founded in 1865, Ave Maria Press is a ministry of the United States Province of Holy Cross.

www.avemariapress.com

Paperback: ISBN-13 978-1-64680-413-9

E-book: ISBN-13 978-1-64680-414-6

Cover image © Getty Images

Cover and text design by Christopher D. Tobin.

Printed and bound in the United States of America.

This devotional is dedicated to my wife, Rachel Bulman, and to my dearest friend Fr. Blake Britton. Thank you both for seeing something in me that I could not yet see and having the love and charisma to help me foster it.

Acknowledgments

Thank you to my children for always loving me, even when I fail to be a good father, and for your patience in allowing me to love God's people in the way I have been called. You will always hold my heart in your hands.

Thank you to my parents for raising me to experience the unconditional love of the Father through your unfailing love and support. Thank you for raising me to encounter the Lord Jesus Christ in his one, holy Catholic Church. I could never express my love enough to you both.

Thank you to Bishop John Noonan for trusting me with the Sacrament of Holy Orders, and to all those who formed me in my diaconate program, especially Deacon Joe Gassman and Deacon Dave Camous.

Thank you to the countless young adults who have honored me by coming and sharing your lives with my family in our home. You give my heart hope for the future of the Church.

Introduction

The Church ends her liturgical year with the celebration of Christ the King, and the following Sunday, we find ourselves officially beginning anew with the season of Advent. Every ending is the chance for a new beginning, and it is my hope that this book can help you do just that—that is, to start anew and to resolve to do better, to turn away from the same vices that have perhaps been dragging you down for years, and to keep your mind's eye fixed on Jesus Christ, who alone can offer you the lasting peace and joy that your heart was made for.

The season of Advent is a time of preparation and therefore a time to examine your Conscience, to take advantage of the healing that comes with a good Confession, and to reclaim your mind and heart for Christ Jesus. It is a season to focus on the coming of Emmanuel, "God with us," not only at ancient Bethlehem but also in you today, and importantly at the end of time, when he will come in glory. Move forward in hope and joyful anticipation this Advent by actively seeking Jesus through a life of genuine devotion and consistent prayer. Weed out those things that block your relationship with him and keep you complacent, those habits that keep you from being the person you want to be, because God wants you to flourish. With a renewed heart and mind, you can then reflect on your life with clarity of vision and be healed of regret. You can look forward with authentic hope, rid of all fear and anxiety. Advent is a time for letting go of the past and leaning in to the Holy Spirit to begin to ask, "What does *God* want for my life?"

As Christians, we recognize that it is not primarily us who seek God "out there" but rather God who has been seeking us from the beginning, from deep within our hearts. Relationship with the Lord is more of an opening up and a receptivity to his arrival than a going out to him. The Lord proves his love in seeking us to the point of sharing in our humanity by the mystery of his Incarnation. He arrives in our midst every day in the context of the holy Mass and by the mystery of the Eucharist. And he will come again at the end of time when he will claim all of creation for the Father. Christ came at Christmas, he comes now, and he will come again. And the dwelling place he prefers is your very heart.

The psalms constitute a central part of the Church's prayer life and express everything from a joyful song to a sorrowful lament. In the liturgy, we turn to the psalms to guide the Liturgy of the Word at Mass, and they anchor our prayer in the Liturgy of the Hours. Anytime they are read or recited, the Holy Spirit invites us into the love of God and into prayerful contemplation by which we come face-to-face with God, who is Love itself.

Each day, we will spend time together with a verse or two from the psalm for that day's Mass. I will share a brief reflection, followed by a minute (or however long you choose) of silent resting in the Lord. I will provide a simple spiritual exercise for the day and then invite you to close by praying again the psalm verses that opened the devotion. At the back of the book are printed the full psalm texts for the Sundays and major feasts from Masses for the season. Pray with them as you wish or as the Lord calls you to do.

The pages of this book are nothing compared to the capacity of your own heart. I pray that each day is a starting point for deeper prayer, a building of anticipation, and a greater love for silence and contemplation. In that silence, our Savior waits to be born in your heart anew. May he come to you again and again in the psalms as you learn to joyfully wait for him.

First Week of Advent

† Fill me with Advent peace, Lord Jesus.

I will say, "Peace be within you!"
For the sake of the house of the LORD our God,
I will seek your good. (Ps 122:8–9)

The word *advent* comes from the Latin *adventus*, which means "arrival." No matter what our lives look like, most of us seem to always be waiting for the arrival of someone or something. Whether it is as ordinary as waiting in the car line to pick up our kids or as profound as waiting to discover our vocation in life, we are always waiting and watching for an arrival. This fundamental aspect of our lives springs from hearts that God has made for the infinite. Our hearts simply cannot come to rest in the passing things of this life.

The Church, in acknowledging this, sets aside these days of Advent, which beckon us to reflect on and pray for that for which we most deeply long: the peace of Christ, a peace beyond all telling. This holy season prepares us to welcome Christ, not just in the profound and beautiful memory of his holy birth long ago at Bethlehem but also in our hearts and homes and in all those we know as neighbors.

Rest for a bit in silence with the Lord.

Think of someone you will likely encounter today. How will you show them peace?

I will say, "Peace be within you!"
For the sake of the house of the LORD our God,
I will seek your good.

† Fill me with Advent peace, Lord Jesus. Amen.

First Week of Advent

† Fill me with Advent peace, Lord Jesus.

I was glad when they said to me,
"Let us go to the house of the Lord!" (Ps 122:1)

In the second chapter of Ephesians, St. Paul tells those to whom he writes at Ephesus that they are "fellow citizens with the holy ones and members of the household of God." We understand this to be true of us as well: *We* belong to the household of God, the Church. How often do we truly rejoice in this amazing truth?

The Church, like Christ, is both human and divine. With the Holy Spirit as her center, the Church is called to stand as a source of unity and consolation in a world tragically divided. In her deepest nature, the Church is not primarily administrator or judge, but mother. As such, she offers a safe haven. She beckons us to come and find comfort in her arms as we lay our heads in her lap. Mother Church washes us clean in the waters of Baptism and feeds us with bread of the finest wheat. She listens to us and offers us healing as she reminds us that we are her beloved children. She will inspire and encourage us to take our places among the holy ones, becoming the saints we are called to become by offering our gifts for the salvation of the world.

Rest for a bit in silence with the Lord.

Write down a list of all the ways in which you have known the Church as a loving mother. Rejoice and give praise for these precious gifts.

I was glad when they said to me,
"Let us go to the house of the Lord!"

† Fill me with Advent peace, Lord Jesus. Amen.

First Week of Advent

† Fill me with Advent peace, Lord Jesus.

In his days may righteousness flourish,
and peace abound, till the moon be no more! (Ps 72:7)

We tend to think of laws as something outside of ourselves that restrict our freedom or take something from us. We make our highest value the ability to make unrestricted choices or to do whatever we please. We reduce truth to something every person is free to decide for themselves. However, classically understood, truth goes beyond our opinions and exists as a reality that we come to discover. Only when we come to discover the truth are we set free from mistakes that blind us.

Just laws are signposts that steer us toward discovery and bring clarity of sight. The truly just people are thus those who allow God's law to mold and conform their hearts to the One who stands as their origin. The just spontaneously give to God what is his due and to others what is theirs. Jesus, as fully God and fully human, is the truly just one who reveals to us the full potential of our humanity. It is Christ, the Law made flesh, that reveals what it is to be fully alive and live as truly free.

Rest for a bit in silence with the Lord.

In what specific ways are you allowing God's law to mold you this Advent? Ask the Lord for the courage to accept his law.

In his days may righteousness flourish,
and peace abound, till the moon be no more!

† Fill me with Advent peace, Lord Jesus. Amen.

First Week of Advent

† Fill me with Advent peace, Lord Jesus.

The LORD is my shepherd, I shall not want;
he makes me lie down in green pastures.
He leads me beside still waters;
he restores my soul. (Ps 23:1–3)

Likely the most familiar and beloved of all the psalms, Psalm 23 has the incredible ability to touch our deepest hearts and remind us of our true identity in Christ. You and I and all people were created to journey in lush or *verdant* pastures along the soothing waters of a restful stream. We were created for a peace that comes only from the Lord, who is our shepherd, always giving us shelter and a place to rest.

We are meant to deeply understand and accept ourselves as sons and daughters of our heavenly Father. And from this child-like freedom comes the capacity to respond from the heart to the beauty and goodness all around us. "It is for freedom that you were set free," St. Paul reminds us in Galatians. How little do we see people taste such freedom! And yet, this is the proper state of each and every human being—to look at life with the eyes of a child, convinced, as it were, that all this abundant goodness of the earth and the bounty of God's love was created for you and for me.

Rest for a bit in silence with the Lord.

Set aside today the things that keep you from walking with the Lord in joy and freedom.

The LORD is my shepherd, I shall not want;
he makes me lie down in green pastures.
He leads me beside still waters;
he restores my soul.

† Fill me with Advent peace, Lord Jesus. Amen.

First Week of Advent

† Fill me with Advent peace, Lord Jesus.

> It is better to take refuge in the LORD
> than to put confidence in man.
> It is better to take refuge in the LORD
> than to put confidence in princes. (Ps 118:8–9)

From the time we are born until old age, you and I need someone. No matter how we might try, we cannot overcome being dependent. Any semblance of self-sufficiency we think we have is an illusion. As St. Paul asks in 1 Corinthians, "What have you that you did not receive?" (4:7). Even our accomplishments are possible only because we were first given life, our gifts, and the cooperation of others. And no matter what we do, nothing of this world is guaranteed to last—not material wealth, jobs, or even our health.

So how are we to respond to this existential crisis?

The secret lies in the very fabric of our being. We are created for relationship, and only in the context of mutual self-gift can we truly discover who we are. Do not be afraid of your dependency; even Jesus depended on other human beings and wholeheartedly entrusted himself to the Father. Depending on—trusting in—the Lord is the only way our hearts will ever find true rest.

Rest for a bit in silence with the Lord.

Today, try abandoning any resentment you may have about having to depend on others into the hands of the Lord.

> It is better to take refuge in the LORD
> than to put confidence in man.
> It is better to take refuge in the LORD
> than to put confidence in princes.

† Fill me with Advent peace, Lord Jesus. Amen.

First Week of Advent

† **Fill me with Advent peace, Lord Jesus.**

One thing have I asked of the LORD,
that will I seek after;
that I may dwell in the house of the LORD
all the days of my life,
to behold the beauty of the LORD
and to inquire in his temple. (Ps 27:4)

At life's greatest moments, there is a certain silence, a "beholding." The moments when I first gazed upon my children's faces the beauty of each one's face were profound gifts of beholding.

Such moments go beyond words because they are, in fact, transcendent. They point beyond themselves to the beauty, truth, and goodness that underlie being itself. They touch us in the deepest depths of our souls because this beholding is an experience of the overwhelming presence of God acting in and through his creation. Catholic Tradition tells us that the highest level of prayer is mystical contemplation, in which the greatest activity of a human person is revealed: to silently and reverently behold the God of the universe and to choose him as our greatest good.

Rest for a bit in silence with the Lord.

Today, make time to be still, behold the beauty around you, and praise God.

One thing have I asked of the LORD,
that will I seek after;
that I may dwell in the house of the LORD
all the days of my life,
to behold the beauty of the LORD
and to inquire in his temple.

† **Fill me with Advent peace, Lord Jesus. Amen.**

First Week of Advent

† Fill me with Advent peace, Lord Jesus.

The LORD builds up Jerusalem;
he gathers the outcasts of Israel.
He heals the brokenhearted,
and binds up their wounds. (Ps 147:2–3)

As a young man, I often found the sufferings of this world overwhelming. Subtle despair lurked in the depths of my soul, ready to suggest that I was not safe. I was discouraged by the world's inability to offer me lasting happiness or meaning. What I was struggling with were the most fundamental questions every person has to ask: What is the meaning of this life in light of such suffering? Is this life good and worth living? And most important, am I loved?

These questions have only been, and could only be, answered adequately by one person in human history: Jesus Christ, God himself made flesh. It is only by encountering Christ that our restless hearts find true peace. Such is the real significance of the word *advent*. The mystery of the Incarnation reveals to us a God who can be trusted, a world that is transcendently beautiful, and the innate dignity of our humanity. Christ is the answer to our despair and the healing of our deepest wounds.

Rest for a bit in silence with the Lord.

Today, give to Jesus what discourages you or causes you to despair. Trust that he will bind up your wounds and remain with you always.

The LORD builds up Jerusalem;
he gathers the outcasts of Israel.
He heals the brokenhearted,
and binds up their wounds.

† Fill me with Advent peace, Lord Jesus. Amen.

Second Week of Advent

† Our God will come to save us!

In his days may righteousness flourish,
and peace abound, till the moon be no more. (Ps 72:7)

Justice, in perhaps the simplest terms, may be defined as giving to another person what is owed to them. This understanding of justice, echoed in the teachings of Aristotle, Cicero, and Thomas Aquinas, means that in our relationship with God, you and I are due little, if anything, other than separation from his presence. The offense we give to God when we sin is infinite because he is infinite and we owe him our entire existence. And yet, the Lord shows us there is something greater than strict justice, something that goes beyond it and exceeds all expectations: mercy.

So much is mercy a part of who God is that he put it on full display when he took our sin upon himself in order to save us and set us free. This overwhelming mercy shown to me personally becomes the piercing truth that causes in me a softening of the heart, an assurance of security, and a desire to love others in freedom. God's mercy informs and sets the standard for how I now give to others the mercy they are due as children of our just and merciful God.

Rest for a bit in silence with the Lord.

Reflect on when you have let yourself experience the mercy and love of Jesus. Have you allowed that mercy to change how you see and treat your neighbor?

In his days may righteousness flourish,
and peace abound, till the moon be no more.

† Our God will come to save us! Amen.

Immaculate Conception of the Blessed Virgin Mary

† Our God will come to save us!

The LORD has made known his victory,
he has revealed his vindication in the sight of the nations. (Ps 98:2–3)

It is an incredible thing to ponder the fact that God has chosen to talk not only directly to us but also through us. To say it more poetically, his preferred language is the flesh. In the person of Jesus Christ, we see that God has chosen to speak with us by becoming one of us in a language we can hear, touch, and taste. God chose to dwell among us, as one of us, born of Mary, who was conceived free of the mark of original sin. In Jesus we know both the love of the Father and the fullness of what it is to be a human. Such love and respect God has for us!

Today we celebrate not only this love but also an overwhelming joy that he has continued to dwell with us through his Body, the Church, among whom the Blessed Virgin Mary holds primacy of place. By leaving his divine plan of redemption dependent upon her free response to becoming the mother of Jesus and therefore the mother of the Church, he shows us that he has gone so far as to *need* us for the salvation of the world.

Rest for a bit in silence with the Lord.

In what areas do you believe Christ is depending on you to help bring about true justice and fulfill the Father's plan of salvation?

The LORD has made known his victory,
he has revealed his vindication in the sight of the nations.

† Our God will come to save us! Amen.

Second Week of Advent

† Our God will come to save us!

Declare his glory among the nations,
his marvelous works among all the peoples! . . .
Say among the nations, "The LORD reigns!" (Ps 96:3, 10)

I used to think of history merely as a recounting of various individuals desperately living out their circumstances in a world full of endless struggle. History seemed to be the intertwining of billions of stories of human beings forging their own ways and identities through their own achievements. I presumed that humanity had progressed over many millennia, eventually leading to my contemporary life. But the measure of that growth cannot be reduced to advances in industry, culture, government, science, technology, or even religious practice. I have now come to know that beginning with the people of Israel and culminating in the person of Jesus Christ, all of history has to be seen anew. Our story finds meaning only in light of a desperate efforts of a Father to draw his beloved children back to himself. To unite our humanity with the Father's divinity is the real meaning of history: the communion of human and divine in the person of Jesus Christ. Only in him do we see the true meaning of our existence.

Rest for a bit in silence with the Lord.

What spiritual practices can you use to contemplate the mystery of God becoming human in Jesus?

Declare his glory among the nations,
his marvelous works among all the peoples! . . .
Say among the nations, "The LORD reigns!"

† Our God will come to save us!

Second Week of Advent

† Our God will come to save us!

The LORD is merciful and gracious,
slow to anger and abounding in mercy. . . .
He does not deal with us according to our sins,
nor repay us according to our iniquities. (Ps 103:8, 10)

One of the hardest spiritual and psychological lessons I've had to learn as an adult is to let go of the desire to *earn* the affection of others. When this mindset dictates our actions, we tend to project that same approach onto our relationship with God. Even those of us blessed with parents who love us unconditionally quickly come to realize that the rest of the world does not love us so. I knew that one day I wanted a family, and that meant bearing the responsibility for taking care of them. The need to achieve became a source of anxiety and shaped how I defined my worth as a person.

But God doesn't want me or you to earn his affection. God is not like the world but the author of it. God loves us no matter what. We are not defined by our limitations or sins in the eyes of God. We are defined by his love for us. He is the one who gets to define who you are. And he says, like any good father, that you are the most lovely thing he's ever seen.

Rest for a bit in silence with the Lord.

Do you define yourself by God's unconditional love for you or by your failures? How can you more fully embrace God's love?

The LORD is merciful and gracious,
slow to anger and abounding in mercy. . . .
He does not deal with us according to our sins,
nor repay us according to our iniquities.

† Our God will come to save us! Amen.

Second Week of Advent

† Our God will come to save us!

All your works shall give thanks to you, O Lord,
and all your saints shall bless you!
They shall speak of the glory of your kingdom,
and tell of your power. (Ps 145:10–11)

When a person encounters Jesus in a profound and life-changing way, an urgent need to speak about it and a desire to act on it emerge. When we genuinely encounter Jesus, the fundamental way that we understand our lives and who we are changes and opens us to vistas of joy that go beyond words. And yet we are compelled to use words to tell others of the love we have experienced so that they too might share in it. With this experience comes a new identity and, therefore, new activity because when God shows you who you are, it comes with a mission. This is what is meant by *evangelization*: to simply allow this Good News to *in-form* you, which in turn can *in-form* all your activity. Since God's invitation to love him in return necessarily encapsulates your whole life, everything you do can be directed to the one whom your heart has come to love above all things. Your love for him has the capacity to move mountains!

Rest for a bit in silence with the Lord.

Are you timid about sharing your encounters with the Lord, or have you been able to share the joy you've found? In what ways can you grow in sharing your faith?

All your works shall give thanks to you, O Lord,
and all your saints shall bless you!
They shall speak of the glory of your kingdom,
and tell of your power.

† Our God will come to save us! Amen.

Feast of Our Lady of Guadalupe

† Our God will come to save us!

O daughter, you are blessed by the Most High God
above all women on earth;
and blessed be the Lord God,
who created the heavens and the earth. (Jdt 13:18)

It is easy to see in this passage from Judith an image of our Blessed Mother, whom we honor today. Mary points us to the purity of divine love, lasting hope, and heavenly glory. Hidden within this young mother, vulnerable and without earthly power, God chose to dwell. God chooses those with little earthly esteem to humble the proud and, in so doing, reveals the true nature of power.

God, who is all-powerful, is also love itself. Power that asserts itself in order to dominate another is not power at all but a disguised weakness. In the end, such power will cease to exist and will bring shame to those who wield it. In God, every act of authority or power is directed in love toward the service of the other, and it is precisely this disposition to love that imbues the Virgin Mary with power and glory in heaven. It is only when we lay our lives down in love for other people that we begin to exercise any true power.

Rest for a bit in silence with the Lord.

Consider the example and intercession of our Blessed Mother and the saints. How can you better adopt their understanding and use of power?

O daughter, you are blessed by the Most High God
above all women on earth;
and blessed be the Lord God,
who created the heavens and the earth.

† Our God will come to save us! Amen.

Second Week of Advent

† Our God will come to save us!

Give ear, O shepherd of Israel! . . .
You who are enthroned upon the cherubim, shine forth! . . .
Stir up your might! . . .
Then we will never turn back from you;
give us life, and we will call on your name! (Ps 80:1, 2, 18)

In the season of Advent, we look back to the child Jesus, and immediately our hearts are filled with love and adoration. In the powerful biblical images of his birth at Bethlehem, we come to see that evil is overcome with a self-sacrificing love embodied in the meekness and vulnerability of a mother and her newborn baby, rather than with violence and destruction. This looking back toward Bethlehem during Advent causes us to reflexively look forward in hope to Christ's Second Coming, when time will give way to eternity. At a spiritual level, this looking forward feels like a deep longing to be brought ever closer into the arms of the one we love. This beautiful and consoling tension within our soul bespeaks the presence of the Holy Spirit, who is teaching us how to pray in ways that go beyond words. As Pope Benedict XVI taught us, "Praying is nothing more than becoming a longing for God."

Rest for a bit in silence with the Lord.

Today, how can you foster longing within your heart for the Lord?

Give ear, O shepherd of Israel! . . .
You who are enthroned upon the cherubim, shine forth! . . .
Stir up your might! . . .
Then we will never turn back from you;
give us life, and we will call on your name!

† Our God will come to save us! Amen.

Sunday, December 14

Third Week of Advent

† **Lord, come and save us!**

[Happy is he] whose hope is in the LORD his God, . . .
who executes justice for the oppressed,
who gives food to the hungry.
The LORD sets the prisoners free. (Ps 146:5, 7)

When Jesus speaks of his coming to call not the righteous but sinners, he is implying not that some people have no need of his saving help but rather that only those who acknowledge their need for him are disposed to actually receive it. God cannot heal our brokenness if we are unwilling to admit we are broken. The "sinners" Jesus came for include all of us, but only the humble admit their helplessness.

The word *humility* comes from the Latin *humus*, meaning "soil," and so indicates those who are "well-grounded" in reality. The poor, the broken, the hungry, and the oppressed are, in a sense, "blessed" because their suffering keeps them from pride and in touch with the deepest truth, namely, that we need God in every way and for everything. He holds us in existence at every moment, and without him we can do nothing. Do not be afraid of your dependency; it is the key to obtaining his grace.

Rest for a bit in silence with the Lord.

How can you get better at letting Jesus into the deepest recesses of your heart where you bury your wounds?

[Happy is he] whose hope is in the LORD his God, . . .
who executes justice for the oppressed,
who gives food to the hungry.
The LORD sets the prisoners free.

† **Lord, come and save us! Amen.**

Third Week of Advent

Make me to know your ways, O Lord;
teach me your paths.
Lead me in your truth, and teach me,
for you are the God of my salvation. (Ps 25:4–5)

With so many choices facing us each day, it's hard to know just *how* to make decisions. Even with the best intentions, such as raising our children to know God and develop virtue, or when all the choices are good, choosing can be daunting. It's easy to get stuck and feel discouraged rather quickly. So, what's the answer?

St. Thomas Aquinas tells us that what we need is wisdom—a gift from God that allows us to comprehend the most foundational levels of reality and to make good choices based on what we understand. We are called to become lovers of wisdom, or *philosophers* (*philo* = love, *Sophia* = wisdom). The book of Proverbs teaches us that "fear of the Lord is the beginning of wisdom" (9:10). In other words, all of our moral decisions and intellectual pursuits must begin with us on our knees, hearts open, and confident that the Lord of the universe will lead us to truth.

Rest for a bit in silence with the Lord.

What choices are you facing today? Give them to the Lord in prayer and wait for wisdom to guide you.

Make me to know your ways, O Lord;
teach me your paths.
Lead me in your truth, and teach me,
for you are the God of my salvation.

† **Lord, come and save us! Amen.**

Third Week of Advent

The LORD is near to the brokenhearted,
and saves the crushed in spirit. (Ps 34:19)

Reflecting back on my years as a youth and young adult, I can say that I was motivated primarily by a need to be found worthy, successful, and loved. What is so strange is that by all outward appearances, people would have thought I was all those things and that I had it all together. But on the inside, I was filled with shame and insecurity like so many. I chose a college far from my hometown precisely so I could start again where people didn't know me and try to reinvent myself. My second chance proved to be worse than the first because, in my desperation to be accepted, I made decisions that would leave my soul crushed.

Perhaps the person, in all of scripture, I identify with the most is the woman with the alabaster jar who weeps at Jesus's feet, anointing them with her tears and perfumed oil. He then proceeds to tell everyone that it is those who have been forgiven much that love him the deepest. Such is my story. It was in the loving gaze of Jesus Christ that my crushed soul found everything it ever wanted, and it is for this reason that I can't imagine I would ever leave him.

Rest for a bit in silence with the Lord.

Imagine holding in your hands some piece of you that seems broken. When you feel ready, open your hands and ask Jesus to revive your spirit.

The LORD is near to the brokenhearted,
and saves the crushed in spirit.

† **Lord, come and save us! Amen.**

Third Week of Advent

May his name endure for ever,
his fame continue as long as the sun!
May men bless themselves by him,
all nations call him blessed! (Ps 72:17)

The Lord loves all his children and desires "all men to be saved and to come to the knowledge of the truth" (1 Tm 2:4). But he does this only with our cooperation. He created us without us, but he will not save us without us. God's chosen people, the Israelites, were always meant to be saved themselves while simultaneously serving as a conduit of salvation for the rest of the world. "All nations [shall] call him blessed." And this principle is true for us as well. You and I are not our own, and our life is not about us. Like the Israelites of the Old Testament, we become fully who we are only when we make a gift of ourselves to the world. We belong to God and are called to break the habit of turning in on ourselves and instead turn outward in love toward our neighbor. Only then can we begin to live life to the full as our heavenly Father created us to do.

Rest for a bit in silence with the Lord.

In what way can you allow the Lord to shine through you today? What will you do to help people meet Christ when they meet you?

May his name endure for ever,
his fame continue as long as the sun!
May men bless themselves by him,
all nations call him blessed!

† **Lord, come and save us! Amen.**

Third Week of Advent

† Lord, come and save us!

For he delivers the needy when he calls,
and the poor and him who has no helper.
He has pity on the weak and the needy,
and saves the lives of the needy. (Ps 72:12–13)

Hope is something that we all do without having been taught. It is a natural instinct to desire something better in the future, even if it is difficult to obtain. In this life we are all "poor," "weak," and "needy," as the psalmist says. The problem is that, in our lowliness, we don't naturally know in what to place our hope. What is *hoped* for is, by its very nature, seemingly hard to obtain. Thus, we find ourselves settling for a "quick fix" that never seems to satisfy in any lasting or meaningful way. It was for this reason that the Son of God was sent to us. He reveals to us that the deepest longing of our hearts is not some "thing" but *somebody*, that is, a relationship in which I discover myself anew as his beloved. In this way our hope moves from an idea to a person. This is why Jesus Christ came and remains with us in the visible and tangible form of the Eucharist within the bosom of his Body, the Church. In the Eucharist you will find your hope and your salvation.

Rest for a bit in silence with the Lord.

What do you hope for most in this life? Does your hope truly lie in the Lord. If, not what can you do today to shift your hope?

For he delivers the needy when he calls,
and the poor and him who has no helper.
He has pity on the weak and the needy,
and saves the lives of the needy.

† Lord, come and save us! Amen.

Third Week of Advent

† Lord, come and save us!

> I will praise your righteousness, yours alone.
> O God, from my youth you have taught me,
> and I still proclaim your wondrous deeds. (Ps 71:16–17)

The story of my life is only great when it is viewed in the context of a divine plan. This is what makes listening to people's testimonies of God's presence in their lives so captivating. Even the greatest epic novel, *The Lord of the Rings*, is only great because it echoes the one great story that is salvation history. I remember weeping early in my conversion when I read Jeremiah 15:16, because in that moment, I caught a glimpse of the overwhelming dignity God had bestowed on me, having created me out of selfless love in his own image and likeness. It is only when I discovered that I belonged to him that I came to know who I truly am. The beauty of this life is almost too much to bear. My life is not about me, and that's a good thing. I will proclaim God's wondrous deeds!

Rest for a bit in silence with the Lord.

What can you do today to tell or show others the wondrous things God has done in your life?

> I will praise your righteousness, yours alone.
> O God, from my youth you have taught me,
> and I still proclaim your wondrous deeds.

† Lord, come and save us! Amen.

Third Week of Advent

† Lord, come and save us!

> Who shall ascend the hill of the LORD?
> And who shall stand in his holy place?
> He who has clean hands and a pure heart,
> who does not lift up his soul to what is false. (Ps 24:3–4)

When I began to read St. John of the Cross as a young adult, I knew that he had experienced, just as I had, the vastness of a world yet to be discovered as one grows closer to God. Anyone who has experienced deep spiritual consolation in prayer quickly realizes how it far surpasses any sensual pleasures. Feeling close to God is what your heart, mind, and soul are meant for, and you can come to know that only by experiencing it. But growing in prayer means you have to actively strive to rid yourself of those sins that you love. And likewise, you cannot stop those habitual sins without regular prayer. What you do in your external life has to match your interior life and vice versa. Such, I have found, is the nature of ascending the mountain of the Lord.

Rest for a bit in silence with the Lord.

Does your external or active life match your life of prayer? If not, what is one thing you can do today to bring a closer balance?

> Who shall ascend the hill of the LORD?
> And who shall stand in his holy place?
> He who has clean hands and a pure heart,
> who does not lift up his soul to what is false.

† Lord, come and save us! Amen.

Sunday, December 21

Fourth Week of Advent

† Let the Lord enter; he is King of glory!

The earth is the LORD's and the fulness thereof,
the world and those who dwell therein;
for he has founded it upon the seas,
and established it upon the rivers. (Ps 24:1–2)

It is interesting to me how many people I have encountered who equate experiencing God's presence with being out in nature. I think there is something very right about that intuition. Early one morning, my wife and I found our ten-year-old son alone on the back porch of a cabin in the mountains. He was praying. When he finished and saw us, he explained, halfway embarrassed, that he was excited to go out early in the silence and beauty of the mountains because God's voice was "much louder up here."

We often forget how much God loves his creation and has left his mark upon it as a means for us to encounter his goodness, truth, and beauty. We are the crown of his creation, made in his image and likeness. And he has bestowed on us the ability to sanctify the natural world by leading it, in the worship of its Creator. Such is the common priesthood of the laity, called to sanctify the mundane by drawing it up into the worship of almighty God.

Rest for a bit in silence with the Lord.

Try to get outside today. Breathe deeply. Respond to God's presence in a prayer of gratitude. Linger as long as you are able.

The earth is the LORD's and the fulness thereof,
the world and those who dwell therein;
for he has founded it upon the seas,
and established it upon the rivers.

† Let the Lord enter; he is King of glory! Amen.

Monday, December 22
Fourth Week of Advent

† Let the Lord enter; he is King of glory!

> The LORD kills and brings to life;
> he brings down to Sheol and raises up.
> The LORD makes poor and makes rich,
> he brings low, he also exalts. (1 Sm 2:6–7)

Human beings are by nature not self-sufficient. As children, we are so utterly dependent that relying on another for essentially every aspect of our survival is of no conscious concern. But in later youth and certainly as adults, many of us become control freaks who strive to forge our own physical, psychological, and spiritual security. Not until I realized that the Lord is literally holding me in existence at every moment of every day did I begin to see that the Lord was in control of my life. Everything that happens to me must pass through God's permissive will. Because of Christ, every circumstance holds the potential to make me a saint. If I accept my suffering as the will of God and give thanks for all the gifts he has given me, that will help make me a saint. Whether we live or die, we can be close to God. As St. Paul reminds us in Romans 8:28, all things work for good for those who love God and entrust themselves to his divine care.

Rest for a bit in silence with the Lord.

What is pressuring you today, and how will you submit it the will of God? Make a simple plan for letting go.

> The LORD kills and brings to life;
> he brings down to Sheol and raises up.
> The LORD makes poor and makes rich,
> he brings low, he also exalts.

† Let the Lord enter; he is King of glory! Amen.

Fourth Week of Advent

† Let the Lord enter; he is King of glory!

Make me to know your ways, O LORD;
teach me your paths.
Lead me in your truth, and teach me,
for you are the God of my salvation. (Ps 25:4–5)

It was Mary's receptivity to God acting in her life that allowed the Word to become incarnate in her womb. This receptive disposition is a necessary freedom of spirit that allows God to act in our lives. In my experience, being closed off to God and his Word goes hand in hand with an openness to the lies of a world fallen into selfishness and sin. Openness to the world brought me nothing but confusion, shame, and despair. This is the enslaving reality of sin: If we give it the opportunity to take root, it darkens our minds to hope. Once committed, sin compels the will to invest fully in fleeting pleasures that let us down while filling us with shame and convinces us that God no longer wants us. We grow convinced that we are all alone in our sin and learn to keep quiet so that others cannot see how pathetic we are. God is constantly loving us, asking us to be open to his healing our wounds and making us whole. All we have to do is trust him, and he will take it from there.

Rest for a bit in silence with the Lord.

Do you feel ready to welcome Christ anew into your heart, mind, and actions? What can you do today to prepare for him?

Make me to know your ways, O LORD;
teach me your paths.
Lead me in your truth, and teach me,
for you are the God of my salvation.

† Let the Lord enter; he is King of glory! Amen.

Christmas Eve

† Let the Lord enter; he is King of glory!

He shall cry to me, "You are my Father,
my God, and the Rock of my salvation." . . .
My merciful love I will keep for him for ever,
and my covenant will stand firm for him. (Ps 89:26, 28)

The birth of the Savior is the Father's definitive yes to keep his promise of faithfulness to his people. And Jesus's faithfulness to do the Father's will by his sacrifice on the Cross is his definitive yes to the Father. We need the absolute faithfulness of a loving Father—to know that. God loves us for whom he has created us to be and will never stop seeking our love in return. This love makes me bound to him and him bound to me. This truth is what changed my whole perspective on life some years ago. It is what allows me to make the shift from being turned in on myself in sorrow and fear to being turned outward in joy and hope. It is only in the absolute faithfulness of the Father, which we come to know in the mystery of the Incarnation, and the absolute faithfulness of the Son, which we come to know in the Paschal Mystery—the death and resurrection of Jesus—that we have access to a joy and hope that never have to leave our hearts.

Rest for a bit in silence with the Lord.

Ponder God's immense love for you and those you love. How can you let this great gift shape your celebration of Christmas?

He shall cry to me, "You are my Father,
my God, and the Rock of my salvation." . . .
My merciful love I will keep for him for ever,
and my covenant will stand firm for him.

† Let the Lord enter; he is King of glory! Amen.

Christmas Day

† Let the heavens be glad and the earth rejoice!

Declare his glory among the nations,
his marvelous works among all the peoples! (Ps 96:3)

What does it mean that God *can* become human? What does it mean that God *did* become human? It would take a whole library to even begin unraveling all that this says about God's divinity and our humanity. When I help others begin to unpack the mystery of the Incarnation, lives are changed in profound ways. Spiritually and psychologically, they begin to grasp not only the depth of God's self-emptying love for us and all of creation but also the innate goodness of that creation, especially the human person.

In Jesus Christ, God has affirmed the intrinsic beauty of our humanity and, by extension, all the material world. Although we were born into sin, sin is not something that is natural to us. It is, in fact, *against our nature* to sin. We are created innately good and *for* the good. And even when we sin, it's usually because we wrongly chose something we think is good for us. When we make God our greatest good, all the goods of this world find their right place in our heart and we love them freely in God. Christ brings all creation—most especially us—back into right order.

Rest for a bit in silence with the Lord.

As we celebrate the great mystery of the Incarnation today, contemplate what it says about who God is and who you are as a child of the Father and disciple of Christ Jesus.

Declare his glory among the nations,
his marvelous works among all the peoples!

† Let the heavens be glad and the earth rejoice! Amen.

Feast of St. Stephen, First Martyr

† Let the heavens be glad and the earth rejoice!

Let your face shine on your servant;
save me in your merciful love! (Ps 31:16)

It is no mistake that we celebrate the feast of St. Stephen, our first martyr, the day after Christmas. In doing so, Holy Mother Church is helping us to align the whole of our lives with our faith. If the Incarnation is true, if Jesus Christ is God in the flesh, then I *must* give my whole heart, mind, and soul to him, even if it costs me my life, as it did St. Stephen. The Incarnation is not a truth that I claim but one that claims me. It leads me on the path of salvation by way of the Cross. After many years of trusting in the world, I came finally to sorrow and despair. But the moment I began to trust in Christ, I discovered joy and hope and peace everlasting. These gifts are worth everything to anyone who has lived in the darkness. Jesus Christ alone is the answer to the longings of the human heart. It is in the Incarnation that we find real meaning. Do not be afraid to be the saint that God has called you to be. Give your life to the one who alone can save.

Rest for a bit in silence with the Lord.

Do a quick search of St. Stephen to learn his story. Choose one act of sacrificial love to do today for the sake of spreading the Gospel.

Let your face shine on your servant;
save me in your merciful love!

† Let the heavens be glad and the earth rejoice! Amen.

Feast of St. John, Apostle and Evangelist

† Let the heavens be glad and the earth rejoice!

Light dawns for the righteous,
and joy for the upright in heart.
Rejoice in the Lord, O you righteous,
and give thanks to his holy name! (Ps 97:11–12)

St. John the apostle often refers to himself as "the disciple whom Jesus loved." This is not necessarily because he believed himself loved more than others but because this is how Jesus's love makes you feel. His loving gaze is so intensely personal and completely fulfilling that it is as if it were directed at you and for you alone. The Lord loves you as if you were his only beloved and would have suffered all he did on the Cross just for you. He leaves the ninety-nine sheep to find the one. There is more rejoicing in heaven over one repentant sinner than over an abundance of the righteous. His love is not "in general," or cumulative, but reckless and passionate for each one of us. Absolute vulnerability and self-gift comprise the nature of the love of God. In some ways, St. John will conclude, the entire Gospel can be reduced to one word: love.

Rest for a bit in silence with the Lord.

Reflect on how you understand God's love for you. Is it personal or just an idea? How has it changed as you've grown older?

Light dawns for the righteous,
and joy for the upright in heart.
Rejoice in the Lord, O you righteous,
and give thanks to his holy name!

† Let the heavens be glad and the earth rejoice! Amen.

Feast of the Holy Family of Jesus, Mary, and Joseph

† **Let the heavens be glad and the earth rejoice!**

> Your wife will be like a fruitful vine
> within your house;
> your children will be like olive shoots
> around your table. (Ps 128:3)

When young, I fell so in love with Jesus that I thought I must become a priest. This caused unrest in my heart because I was already dating my future wife. I didn't recognize that God established marriage and the family as the normative path to holiness. Family life is built into the very fabric of our human nature and is meant to be a school of self-gift and holiness. The most beautiful lesson I have learned is what John Paul II referred to as the *law of gift*; namely, the more I live my life for the sake of my wife and kids, the more I know true joy. Selfishness only leaves me unsatisfied and enslaved. The Holy Family represents true freedom and joy because in their mutual gift to one another, they become who they were called to be and share in the ever-dynamic love of God.

Rest for a bit in silence with the Lord.

Do your family relationships need to be redeemed? Pray today for the wisdom to kindle change or in gratitude for the gift of your family.

> Your wife will be like a fruitful vine
> within your house;
> your children will be like olive shoots
> around your table!

† **Let the heavens be glad and the earth rejoice! Amen.**

Fifth Day in the Octave of Christmas

† Let the heavens be glad and the earth rejoice!

The LORD made the heavens.
Honor and majesty are before him;
strength and beauty are in his sanctuary. (Ps 96:5–6)

In my pursuit of a life rooted in truth, I can say that what Jesus calls *metanoia* (conversion) is what it's all about. This Greek term literally means to go beyond the confines of your own mind and take on the *logic* of the *Logos*—the Word himself: Jesus Christ. Most people subconsciously draw a distinction between reality and their faith—relegating God only to the abstract. But this could not be further from the truth. Jesus is the one through whom all things were created. The world is only intelligible inasmuch as it reflects Jesus Christ. All that we have discovered by way of the natural sciences, all our wants and needs, find their origin in him. He is the beginning and end of all things. Until we learn to see reality anew—and I mean in every aspect of our lives—we will not perceive things as they really are. Jesus is the corrective lens to our blurred vision.

Rest for a bit in silence with the Lord.

Consider what areas of your mind and heart are in need of *metanoia*. How can you, in everyday life, learn to understand the world more clearly by holding Christ at the center?

The LORD made the heavens.
Honor and majesty are before him;
strength and beauty are in his sanctuary.

† Let the heavens be glad and the earth rejoice! Amen.

Sixth Day in the Octave of Christmas

† Let the heavens be glad and the earth rejoice!

Say among the nations, "The LORD reigns!
Yes, the world is established, it shall never be moved;
he will judge the peoples with equity." (Ps 96:10)

Jesus was not shy to call his disciples to greatness. "I came that they may have life, and have it abundantly" (Jn 10:10). I have learned that in order to live life abundantly. I must first be filled myself. The Incarnation offers us a *perspective of fullness*. There is nothing that the Lord Jesus has not redeemed—even our deepest sufferings. Unfortunately, we often act as if this isn't true. When our sufferings dominate our perspective, and we then operate from a place of lack instead of fullness, we despair and often hurt others around us.

The good news is that this perspective is not true! In reality, the God of the universe identifies with the poor and broken. Jesus came not for the healthy but for the sick, not for the righteous but for sinners. I encourage you to own your brokenness and sufferings. Let the Lord show you that he can redeem by grace what you perceive as your greatest suffering or vice and make you whole.

How can you shift your disposition toward everyday life so that you live free from fear and with an abundance of joy and love?

Say among the nations, "The LORD reigns!
Yes, the world is established, it shall never be moved;
he will judge the peoples with equity."

† Let the heavens be glad and the earth rejoice! Amen.

Seventh Day in the Octave of Christmas

† Let the heavens be glad and the earth rejoice!

He comes to judge the earth.
He will judge the world with righteousness,
and the peoples with his truth. (Ps 96:13)

As we continue to celebrate the mystery of the Incarnation during this holy season, it's important to pause and ponder what the Church means by *mystery*. When we call something a mystery, it is not because that reality is unable to be known. Rather, it means that a truth, a reality, is inexhaustibly knowable because it is of God. Mysteries are supranatural, meaning they are realities that exist beyond the natural order. They draw our minds into what they are incapable of grasping without God guiding us by grace. This is the underlying logic of having a liturgical year in which we circle back around and contemplate, over and over again, the mysteries of our faith. Catholic lives are meant to be directed by the liturgy and the cycles and seasons of the liturgical year. Giving our lives over to this pattern of praise and contemplation of the mysteries of God draws us nearer to Christ and toward the perfection of our ever-deepening journey into the heart of God.

Rest for a bit in silence with the Lord.

How you can be more attentive to the liturgical year? Create a plan for growth in this area of Catholic life.

He comes to judge the earth.
He will judge the world with righteousness,
and the peoples with his truth.

† Let the heavens be glad and the earth rejoice! Amen.

Solemnity of Mary, Mother of God

† May the peoples praise you, O God!

Let the nations be glad and sing for joy,
for you judge the peoples with equity
and guide the nations upon earth. (Ps 67:4)

Today we contemplate the mystery of Mary as Mother of God. When I was being interviewed prior to my acceptance into diaconate formation, my wife was asked if she understood that, if I were to be ordained, I would be unable to marry again if she died before me. The interviewer asked if my wife would be bothered that our children might grow up without a mother if by chance she died while they were young. Without missing a beat, my wife responded that they already have another mother and she would be well equipped to handle the situation! Such a statement comes from a woman who has taken the Gospel seriously and has allowed its profound mysteries to penetrate and convert her mind and heart. Mary's motherhood was meant to be not merely a biological function but a deep and lasting spiritual reality. Her submission, her *fiat*—the willingness to let God's will be done in her—was a perfect and permanent assent. Our yes to Jesus is merely an echo of that first yes given by our Mother, who bore Christ to the world.

Rest for a bit in silence with the Lord.

Reflect today on the title "Mary, Mother of God." Contemplate the meaning of this profound mystery. What does it mean to you that *God has a mother*?

Let the nations be glad and sing for joy,
for you judge the peoples with equity
and guide the nations upon earth.

† May the peoples praise you, O God! Amen.

Weekday Before Epiphany

† May the peoples praise you, O God!

O sing to the Lord a new song,
for he has done marvelous things! (Ps 98:1)

During the birth of my oldest child, he suffered an injury that would leave one of his arms permanently disabled. He ended up going through several very long and invasive surgeries beginning around the age of one. There is a unique suffering that occurs in the heart of a father who has to stand helpless before his son as he is thrust into tragedy. To this day, I have trouble accepting it. But the truth is that it is precisely for times like this that Jesus enters into suffering himself to redeem it. Jesus identifies with the poor, the broken, and the suffering. And in so doing, he reveals that our wounds and scars are not a cause for shame but a claim on his own Sacred Heart. Our idea of perfection is not the same as that of the God of the universe, who is perfect in every way. Christ Jesus transforms suffering into new life, and sorrow into joy, if we but allow him into our wounds, where he will save us.

Rest for a bit in silence with the Lord.

Ask yourself today, Do I truly believe there is nothing that the Lord Jesus cannot redeem in my life? Do I live as though I believe this? How might I do better with this?

O sing to the Lord a new song,
for he has done marvelous things!

† May the peoples praise you, O God! Amen.

Weekday Before Epiphany

† May the peoples praise you, O God!

Make a joyful noise to the LORD, all the earth;
break forth into joyous song and sing praises! (Ps 98:4)

St. Thomas Aquinas tells us that there are two ways in which we can find joy in this life. The first is by participating in the love of God. By this, Aquinas means to experience how in love God is with each of us and to then return that love to God. Nevertheless, this participation cannot be perfect in this life because of sin and brokenness in ourselves and in our world. The second and more perfect way to find joy is to love God for his own sake, regardless of how close or far I seem to be from him. This is like the love of a husband for his wife, where he rejoices that she is well taken care of and safe, even if he is being led to his own death. He does not care about his own life as long as he knows that she exists and is secure in love. This is the highest form of love. Losing ourselves in the love of God is the point at which we truly begin to live with freedom. Do not be afraid to lay down your own needs in order to take joy in the fact that our loving God exists. Be joyful simply because God is!

Rest for a bit in silence with the Lord.

Carve out ten or fifteen minutes today to simply be with the Lord. Can you rest in joy simply because God is? If not, how might you grow toward this?

Make a joyful noise to the LORD, all the earth;
break forth into joyous song and sing praises.!

† May the peoples praise you, O God! Amen.

Feast of Epiphany

† Lord, every nation on earth will adore you.

May the kings of Tarshish and of the isles
render him tribute,
may the kings of Sheba and Seba bring gifts!
May the kings fall down before him,
all nations serve him! (Ps 72:10–11)

The three magi were open to the reality of the divine and let their study of the physical naturally lead them to the supernatural. By following the star, the magi—or *wise men*, or *kings*—came to encounter the one "by whom all things were created," Jesus Christ (1 Cor 8:6, NLT). I try to approach all study this way. Even the natural sciences are not opposed to faith. They all lead me to encounter the beauty of the mind of a creator. The desire to know the mind of God set human beings on a path of discovery via every kind of science and gave rise to the university. Unfortunately, today we have often tried to take God out of the picture and, in so doing, have reduced science to a means for manipulation and selfish gain. May this Epiphany allow us to meditate on the star until we find ourselves meditating on the Creator of the stars.

Rest for a bit in silence with the Lord.

How can you adjust your everyday work so that you remain conscious of being in God's presence? Make a plan to do so.

May the kings of Tarshish and of the isles
render him tribute,
may the kings of Sheba and Seba bring gifts!
May the kings fall down before him,
all nations serve him!

† Lord, every nation on earth will adore you. Amen.

Christmas Weekday

† Lord, every nation on earth will adore you.

Ask of me, and I will make the nations your heritage,
and the ends of the earth your possession. (Ps 2:8)

In the biblical telling of the three magi meeting the Christ Child
and paying him homage, we are meant to see the long-awaited
Savior being presented *through* the nation of Israel to the gentiles,
that is, to the whole world. This becomes the pattern of evangelization for all of us. Jesus's love for me is the most personal thing
I've ever experienced. He has healed wounds in the depths of my
soul that most people would not know exist. And yet this salvation, which is so deeply personal, is at the same time something
that God intends for others to accept *through* me. We are saved
not in a vacuum but as a family. God is not "my Father" but "Our
Father, who art in heaven." One sure sign that we are on the path
of salvation is if that love we have come to know in Christ easily
pours out into those around us. This can come about only with a
freeing, yet painful, change in perspective in which we are compelled to let go of ego and give ourselves over to the one we love,
the author of all life. And then—through him and with him and
in him—to all the world.

Rest for a bit in silence with the Lord.

How open are you to loving others freely? What small steps will
you take today to open yourself more fully to this calling of our
faith?

Ask of me, and I will make the nations your heritage,
and the ends of the earth your possession.

† Lord, every nation on earth will adore you. Amen.

Christmas Weekday

† **Lord, every nation on earth will adore you.**

May he defend the cause of the poor of the people,
give deliverance to the needy. . . .
In his days may righteousness flourish,
and peace abound, till the moon be no more! (Ps 72:4, 7)

Of all the people with whom the great news of the Messiah's birth could be shared, it was given to poor and uneducated shepherds. These shepherds appear in stark contrast to the herald angels, who are higher than human beings and immeasurably more intelligent in the order of creation. And here is the point: In Christ, power and authority are turned on their heads. God, who is all-powerful, has taken the form of a helpless infant. And he has made his angels to be at the service of the lowliest of human beings. This means that the power dynamic we are used to in our broken societies exists in contrast to the way God comes to human hearts. No longer should I strive to be a person of authority and influence for the sake of ambition, because Jesus has definitively identified himself with the poor and needy. To seek to escape the reality that I am a helpless sinner in need of God is to separate myself from Jesus, who has united himself with such as these.

Rest for a bit in silence with the Lord.

Who are the poor you encounter each day? How can you draw closer to them and learn from them?

May he defend the cause of the poor of the people,
give deliverance to the needy. . . .
In his days may righteousness flourish,
and peace abound, till the moon be no more! (Ps 72:4, 7)

† **Lord, every nation on earth will adore you. Amen.**

Christmas Weekday

† Lord, every nation on earth will adore you.

For he delivers the needy when he calls,
the poor and him who has no helper.
He has pity on the weak and the needy,
and saves the lives of the needy. (Ps 72:12–13)

As we grow in wisdom, we realize that there is a difference between immortality and eternal life. Length of life means very little without quality of life. The long-awaited Messiah, Jesus Christ, came to show us what it is to truly live. He shows us that salvation is far more than having our fill of endless superficial desires. Salvation is the satiation of our deepest desire—unconditional and ever-deepening love. It turns out not to be a *something*, but a *someone*. As the psalmist reminds us, Jesus Christ saves the weak, the needy, and the afflicted. Salvation comes in discovering that I am loved for who I am and a call to love in return. This is the pearl of great price that, when obtained, makes relative all the other sufferings and joys in this life such that I can learn to reach beyond them because my heart knows what it wants, and indeed it already has it.

Rest for a bit in silence with the Lord.

Reflect on the areas of your life or your self-perception where you experience poverty or weakness. Where do you sense some kind of affliction? Now, turn to Jesus in prayer and release these things to him. Pray that he helps you do this.

For he delivers the needy when he calls,
the poor and him who has no helper.
He has pity on the weak and the needy,
and saves the lives of the needy.

† Lord, every nation on earth will adore you. Amen.

Christmas Weekday

† Lord, every nation on earth will adore you.

Give the king your justice, O God,
and your righteousness to the royal son!
May he judge your people with righteousness,
and your poor with justice! (Ps 72:1–2)

In our psalm today, we hear the plea of a virtuous man begging for the grace of God to help him persevere. You see, asking for help is often mistaken for giving up or even failing. But if we allow ourselves to feel the ache of helplessness, to realize the need for a savior, we are made free to truly know and love the Lord. Although the Christmas season is one for rejoicing and celebrating, it can also be a time when we are reminded of our frailties and short-comings, as can every season. The Lord invites us not to run and hide from these realizations but to be open and vulnerable about them with him. He invites us to trust that he can bring about an even greater good from these human realities if we cooperate with his grace. The wisest people are those who have suffered well and learned from their mistakes by entrusting them to God—in other words, those who begin to plead for the justice of the King.

Rest for a bit in silence with the Lord.

Take time today to be vulnerable with God about your failures and weaknesses. Let the Lord help you to see these failures in the light of his loving gaze and ask him for the grace to see that your need for a savior is your strength.

Give the king your justice, O God,
and your righteousness to the royal son!
May he judge your people with righteousness,
and your poor with justice!

† Lord, every nation on earth will adore you. Amen.

Christmas Weekday

† Lord, every nation on earth will adore you.

Praise the LORD, O Jerusalem!
Praise your God, O Zion!
For he strengthens the bars of your gates; . . .
he fills you with the finest of the wheat. (Ps 147:12, 14)

All things find their origin and fulfillment in Jesus. His birth at Bethlehem marked the fullness of time because history preceding it looked forward to it. And everything since looks back to it in order to understand itself. The Church that Christ founded in the lives and ministry of the apostles continues to bear his presence to the world. In being born at this time in history—after the very meaning of our lives has been born in the flesh and remains with us now in and through his incarnate Body, the Church—we have been given a gift beyond all measure: the grace to encounter Christ personally, accept the faith, and begin to live.

The enemy of our spiritual lives is not suffering but a spirit of indifference and boredom. We must actively fight this temptation with Christian joy, which is the fruit of experiencing the love of God and the thrill of gratitude that comes with recognizing the great gift of the fullness of truth in our Catholic faith.

Rest for a bit in silence with the Lord.

Consider why you are Catholic and give thanks to God for the gifts the Church brings to your life.

Praise the LORD, O Jerusalem!
Praise your God, O Zion!
For he strengthens the bars of your gates; . . .
he fills you with the finest of the wheat.

† Lord, every nation on earth will adore you. Amen.

Christmas Weekday

† Lord, every nation on earth will adore you.

For the LORD takes pleasure in his people;
he adorns the humble with victory.
Let the faithful exult in glory;
let them sing for joy on their couches. (Ps 149:4–5)

The water baptism of Jesus by John in the Jordan River was a sign pointing to his total surrender in sacrificial love through his death on the Cross. By submitting to John's baptism of repentance, Jesus established his identity with the poor and the broken. He has made himself *one* with the repentant sinner who acknowledges his brokenness and turns to God for help. What this means for you and me is that only by embracing our brokenness do we find union with Christ. When I am stuck in pride, I isolate myself from Jesus and salvation. I personally have wasted so much spiritual energy and time, seeking to cover up my weaknesses while vying for the love of those incapable of offering it to me. We have only ever needed someone to love us by entering into our own brokenness. In Christ, we come to see that we are defined not by our mistakes but by the unconditional love of the Father and that we are called to participate in the fullness of his life for all eternity.

Rest for a bit in silence with the Lord.

Are there wounds in your life that limit your freedom? Pray today that you can open those wounds to the healing presence of Christ.

For the LORD takes pleasure in his people;
he adorns the humble with victory.
Let the faithful exult in glory;
let them sing for joy on their couches.

† Lord, every nation on earth will adore you. Amen.

Sunday, January 11
Feast of the Baptism of the Lord

† The Lord is enthroned as king forever.

Ascribe to the LORD, O sons of God,
ascribe to the LORD glory and strength.
Ascribe to the LORD the glory of his name;
worship the LORD in holy attire. (Ps 29:1–2)

In the Catholic Eastern Rite, the Feast of Epiphany focuses on the Baptism of the Lord rather than on the three magi. This is because the Lord's baptism is also an *epiphany*, or striking realization. In the baptism of Jesus, we see not only that the Messiah has come but that he is much more than expected. He is not merely another king or prophet but God himself in the flesh! In the gospel stories of John baptizing Jesus, the Father's voice from heaven claims Jesus as his "beloved Son," and the Holy Spirit hovers over him like a dove, revealing his divinity.

Because Jesus is fully divine *and* fully human, in him, divinity and humanity have become one. This is true for us, too, when we are baptized and the Holy Spirit makes his home within us. In the baptism of Jesus, we begin to perceive the fullness of the Christmas mystery—our perfect, unending communion with God, who is love.

Rest for a bit in silence with the Lord.

Contemplate the mystery of *you* being taken up into the life of the Holy Trinity.

Ascribe to the LORD, O sons of God,
ascribe to the LORD glory and strength.
Ascribe to the LORD the glory of his name;
worship the LORD in holy attire.

† The Lord is enthroned as king forever. Amen.

First Sunday of Advent

Psalm 122

I was glad when they said to me,
"Let us go to the house of the LORD!"
Our feet have been standing
within your gates, O Jerusalem!

Jerusalem, built as a city
which is bound firmly together,
to which the tribes go up,
the tribes of the LORD,
as was decreed for Israel,
to give thanks to the name of the LORD.
There thrones for judgment were set,
the thrones of the house of David.

Pray for the peace of Jerusalem!
"May they prosper who love you!
Peace be within your walls,
and security within your towers!"
For my brethren and companions' sake
I will say, "Peace be within you!"
For the sake of the house of the LORD our God,
I will seek your good.

Second Sunday of Advent

Psalm 72:1–2, 7–8, 12–13, 17

Give the king your justice, O God,
and your righteousness to the royal son!
May he judge your people with righteousness,
and your poor with justice! . . .

In his days may righteousness flourish,
and peace abound, till the moon be no more!

May he have dominion from sea to sea,
and from the River to the ends of the earth! . . .

For he delivers the needy when he calls,
the poor and him who has no helper.
He has pity on the weak and the needy,
and saves the lives of the needy. . . .

May his name endure for ever,
his fame continue as long as the sun!

Third Sunday of Advent

Psalm 146:5–10

[Happy is he] whose hope is in the LORD his God, . . .
who keeps faith for ever;
who executes justice for the oppressed;
who gives food to the hungry.

The LORD sets the prisoners free;
the LORD opens the eyes of the blind.
The LORD lifts up those who are bowed down;
the LORD loves the righteous.
The LORD watches over the sojourners,
he upholds the widow and the fatherless;
but the way of the wicked he brings to ruin.

The LORD will reign for ever,
your God, O Zion, to all generations.
Praise the LORD!

Fourth Sunday of Advent

Psalm 24:1–6

The earth is the LORD's and the fulness thereof,
the world and those who dwell therein;
for he has founded it upon the seas,
and established it upon the rivers.

Who shall ascend the hill of the LORD?
And who shall stand in his holy place?
He who has clean hands and a pure heart,
who does not lift up his soul to what is false,
and does not swear deceitfully.
He will receive blessing from the LORD,
and vindication from the God of his salvation.
Such is the generation of those who seek him,
who seek the face of the God of Jacob.

Christmas Eve
Vigil Mass of Christmas

Psalm 89:4–5, 15–16, 26, 28

"I will establish your descendants for ever,
and build your throne for all generations."

Let the heavens praise your wonders, O LORD,
your faithfulness in the assembly of the holy ones! . . .
Blessed are the people who know the festal shout,
who walk, O LORD, in the light of your countenance,
who exult in your name all the day,
and extol your righteousness. . . .

He shall cry to me, "You are my father,
my God, and the Rock of my salvation." . . .
My merciful love I will keep for him for ever,
and my covenant will stand firm for him.

Christmas Mass at Midnight

Psalm 96:1–3, 11–13

O sing to the LORD a new song;
sing to the LORD, all the earth!
Sing to the LORD, bless his name;
tell of his salvation from day to day.
Declare his glory among the nations,
his marvelous works among all the peoples! . . .

Let the heavens be glad, and let the earth rejoice;
let the sea roar, and all that fills it;
let the field exult, and everything in it!
Then shall all the trees of the wood sing for joy
before the LORD, for he comes,
for he comes to judge the earth.
He will judge the world with righteousness,
and the peoples with his truth.

Christmas Mass at Dawn

Psalm 97:1, 6, 11–12

The LORD reigns; let the earth rejoice;
let the many islands be glad! . . .

The heavens proclaim his righteousness;
and all the peoples behold his glory. . . .

Light dawns for the righteous,
and joy for the upright in heart
Rejoice in the LORD, O you righteous,
and give thanks to his holy name!

Christmas Mass During the Day

Psalm 98:1–6

O sing to the LORD a new song,
for he has done marvelous things!
His right hand and his holy arm
have gotten him victory.
The LORD has made known his victory,
he has revealed his vindication in the sight of the
nations.
He has remembered his mercy and faithfulness
to the house of Israel.
All the ends of the earth have seen
the victory of our God.

Make a joyful noise to the LORD, all the earth;
break forth into joyous song and sing praises!
Sing praises to the LORD with the lyre,
with the lyre and the sound of melody!
With trumpets and the sound of the horn
make a joyful noise before the King, the LORD!

Feast of the Holy Family

Psalm 128:1–5

Blessed is every one who fears the LORD,
who walks in his ways!
You shall eat the fruit of the labor of your hands;
you shall be happy, and it shall be well with you.

Your wife will be like a fruitful vine
within your house;
your children will be like olive shoots
around your table.
Behold, thus shall the man be blessed
who fears the LORD.

The LORD bless you from Zion!
May you see the prosperity of Jerusalem
all the days of your life!

Solemnity of the Epiphany

Psalm 72:1–2, 7–8, 10–13

Give the king your justice, O God,
and your righteousness to the royal son!
May he judge your people with righteousness,
and your poor with justice! . . .

In his days may righteousness flourish,
and peace abound, till the moon be no more!

May he have dominion from sea to sea,
and from the River to the ends of the earth! . . .
May the kings of Tarshish and of the isles
render him tribute,
may the kings of Sheba and Seba bring gifts!
May all kings fall down before him
all nations serve him!

For he delivers the needy when he calls,
the poor and him who has no helper.
He has pity on the weak and the needy,
and saves the lives of the needy.

Feast of the Baptism of the Lord

Psalm 29:1–4, 9–10

Ascribe to the LORD, O sons of God,
ascribe to the LORD glory and strength.
Ascribe to the LORD the glory of his name;
worship the LORD in holy attire.

The voice of the LORD is upon the waters;
the God of glory thunders,
the LORD, upon many waters.
The voice of the LORD is powerful,
the voice of the LORD is full of majesty. . . .

The voice of the LORD makes the oaks to whirl,
and strips the forests bare;
and in his temple all cry, "Glory!"

The LORD sits enthroned over the fold;
the LORD sits enthroned as king for ever.

Jason Bulman is a permanent deacon serving in the diocese of Orlando and a national speaker, writer, and physician assistant.

Bulman earned a master's degree in theology from Saint Leo University.

He has written for the Word on Fire *Evangelization & Culture* journal and cohosts the YouTube video series *Meet the Bulmans*.

Bulman lives in central Florida with his wife, Rachel, and their children.

Instagram: @jason.bulman

Let the Psalms Renew
Your Heart this Lent

Let *Praying with the Psalms* from Emily Mae Mentock
be your daily companion as you walk with
the Lord through the season of Lent.

In just three meaningful minutes each day, you'll be invited
to lay down your burdens, open your heart to God's mercy,
and prepare your soul for the joy of Easter.

EACH DAILY DEVOTION INCLUDES:

- one or two seasonal psalm verses to focus your heart;
- a brief, thoughtful reflection on the meaning behind
  the words;
- a prompt to pause and rest in silence with the Lord;
- a simple spiritual exercise to carry into your day; and
- a return to the psalm verse to end your prayer.

Whether you're beginning a daily prayer habit or seeking
to deepen your Lenten journey, this devotional offers a beautiful
and practical way to encounter God in the sacred poetry
of the psalms—and to be transformed by his Word.